NEWFOUNDLAND

NEWFOUNDLAND

Photography by
BEN HANSEN

Foreword by
Michael Harrington

Vinland Press, St. John's, Newfoundland

Dedicated to Joyce, David, Peter, Jeffrey, Marina,
Colin, Heidi, Sarah and Valerie

Foreword

Ben Hansen's Newfoundland

Post-Confederation Newfoundland has recently become a mecca for the photographer — including those practitioners who regard the camera as a new medium for the visual arts. Up to the Second World War the Island had been a terra incognita in that respect, almost a preserve for a small group of mainly English sportsmen and a fistful of foreigners who, in the late 19th and early 20th centuries, rediscovered its pristine purity.

Attracted by its game-filled woods and barrens, prolific lakes, bounteous ponds and rivers, a number of them with some painting ability had the vision and determination to "lug along" an extra supply load in the shape of the cumbersome photographic equipment of their time. These adventurers included A. Radclyffe Dugmore, of international fame, who was the first to "shoot" the woodland caribou, the Island's mascot, with a camera!

But it belonged to another handful of gifted and painstaking persons, the first of the home-grown commercial photographers and again mainly of English stock, to add to the local pictorial heritage. Men like Lyon, Holloway, Parsons and Vey spent their short summers journeying along the indented coastline or penetrating the trackless hinterland to imprint on glass plates and celluloid the captivating vistas of the old Newfoundland and to keep for today's generation what would otherwise be a treasure of lost quaintness.

So it's not surprising that the photographic renaissance of the 1950s onwards also found the newcomers from Europe as well as mainland Canada in the vanguard. Among them was Ben Hansen, a rugged native of modern Denmark. He and his family of eight fell in love with their new home that presented such a startling contrast to their generally flat and pastoral homeland.

But there was more than just wild seascapes and inland wilderness to remind them of their Scandinavian heritage. It is no mere coincidence that these photos include the reconstructed evidence that the first foothold of the Vikings in North America was made at the northernmost tip of Newfoundland close to one thousand years ago. As well, there is an appreciative awareness of the majesty of the giant headlands and prehistoric rocks along the more remote reaches of the Great Northern Peninsula and on other stretches of the Island's littoral.

Ben Hansen makes no pretence of being a photographic artist; indeed he is more in the mould of the pioneers already noted whose first task was to record what they looked upon though ever so fleetingly; and if the eye of the beholder saw something especially beautiful and appealing in these images then so be it. Despite that disclaimer the Hansen perspective embraces a variety of horizons. His eye has "glanced from heaven to earth" and back again.

He uses the mysterious alchemy of fog and mist to transmute beetling bluffs into creatures of a new Stone Age. Wave-sculptured icebergs rise from the desert of the sea like immaculate Pyramids in their stateliness and the Ancient Mariner's albatross in their fatefulness. The silver thaw at Middle Cove somehow reflects the myriad feathered population of the Bird Rock at Cape St. Mary's; while Cape Spear, the last land between North America and Denmark, is highlighted by a sensitive comparison between a triple triad of wheeling gulls, wallowing bergs and man-made installations for survival. "Yard Art at Piccadilly" seems the quintessence of Newfoundland's original placenames and innovative handicrafts.

Those who might suggest this is merely the tourist's Newfoundland would be in error. There are many pictures that depict facets of the modern community which the earlier devotees would have been glad to know and eager to portray. These include eye-catching scenes of St. John's that have flourished ever since John Cabot's caravel followed the longships to the New Isle.

The Newfoundland capital, the oldest community in North America permanently settled by white men from Europe, is given proper attention. Witness the Battery fishing enclave in the very mouth of the harbour's Narrows on the site of relics of 18th century wars; the almost two century old Fort Amherst Light; a graceful modern yacht at anchor in antique Quidi Vidi; Memorial University's acclaimed Botanical Gardens at Oxen Pond and that institution's own "urban sprawl"; a romantic old home on an exquisite winter morning; a motorist's-eye view of "Lar's Mart", the convenience store par excellence still open for business after midnight.

In short, the more than 100 views in this volume represent a kaleidoscope of colour, wonder and warmth that will remain an unending source of inspiration and delight.

Michael Harrington

Heading out past Fort Amherst at sun up ▷

Port de Grave, Conception Bay

Mending a net at Blackhead North

Fishing gear at La Scie

Port Saunders

Shoe Cove, Green Bay

Dunfield, Trinity Bay

Lines and twines at Petty Harbour

Snooks Arm, Green Bay

Green's Harbour, Trinity Bay

End of a long day, Great Northern Peninsula

Deadman's Cove, Great Northern Peninsula

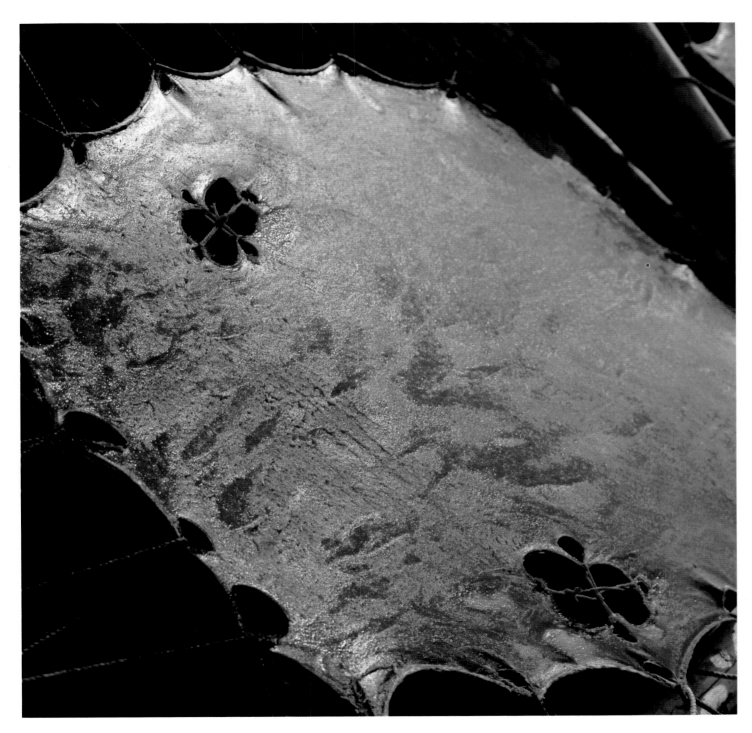

Sealskin drying, Deadman's Cove

Tors Cove

Moore's Cove, Notre Dame Bay

Viking settlement at L'Anse-au-Meadows

A Faering replica built in Norway

PREVIOUS PAGE
Woody Point, Bonne Bay
Norris Point, Bonne Bay

Pitcher Plant

Rattling Brook Falls,
Humber Arm

Twillingate, Notre Dame Bay

Trinity from Gun Hill, Trinity Bay

Norris Point, Bonne Bay

Cook's Harbour, Pistolet Bay

Portugal Cove, Conception Bay

Royal Newfoundland Yacht Club, Long Pond, Conception Bay

Trinity, Trinity Bay

Knights Cove, Bonavista Bay

Little Hearts Ease, Trinity Bay

Gooseberry Cove, Trinity Bay

Greenspond, Bonavista Bay

Tickle Cove, Bonavista Bay

Red Cliff, Bonavista Bay

Winterton, Trinity Bay

Southport, Trinity Bay

Southport, Trinity Bay

Plate Cove, Bonavista Bay

Beachcombing turned into "Yard Art" at
Piccadilly, Port au Port Peninsula

Garden Cove from St. Lunaire, Great Northern Peninsula

"Downers", Greenspond,
Bonavista Bay

Hearts Content, Trinity Bay

Logy Bay

Channel-Port-aux-Basques

Mr. Garland Butt, Channel-Port-aux-Basques

Rencontre East, Belle Bay

On the wharf, Grey River

Grey River

Western Point lighthouse near Francois

Francois

Francois

Cape Spear, the most Easterly point of land in North America

Shenandoah II at Quidi Vidi

Morning fog turns to . . .

Golden sunset at The Battery, St. John's

Twillingate, Notre Dame Bay

Little Harbour, Notre Dame Bay

◁ "Silver Thaw" at Middle Cove

Winter's work at Logy Bay and Petty Harbour

Cape Spear

"Growler" at St. Carol's, Great Northern Peninsula

Flatrock

Trouty, Trinity Bay

Cottrell's Cove, Notre Dame Bay

Cottrell's Cove,
Notre Dame Bay

St. Mary's, St. Mary's Bay

◁ Brigus, Conception Bay

Colinet Cataracts

Botanical Garden at Oxen Pond

Hibb's Cove

South West River

Lumsden North

Joe Batt's Arm, Fogo Island

Holyrood, Conception Bay

◁ Harbour Grace, Conception Bay

Cape St. Mary's bird sanctuary

Cape St. Mary's bird sanctuary ▷

Cape St. Mary's bird sanctuary

Greenspond, Bonavista Bay

Bell Island, Conception Bay

Bell Island, Conception Bay

Carbonear, Conception Bay

New Bonaventure, Trinity Bay

Sandy Cove, Bonavista Bay

Gooseberry Cove, Placentia Bay

St. Phillips, Conception Bay

East Arm, Bonne Bay

Quidi Vidi

Cape Race

Placentia, Placentia Bay

Port Kirwin

St. John's ▷

St. John's, Memorial University in foreground ▷

Queen's Battery, looking towards Cape Spear

Fort Amherst

St. John's at daybreak

"Lar's", still open at midnight

Autumn at Oxen Pond. . .

and at Bowring Park

A beautiful winter morning. . .

quickly turns to an
afternoon snow storm

St. Thomas' Anglican Church,
(The Old Garrison Church) built in 1836

Bannerman House, built in 1849

Inviting glow at Memorial University's R. Gushue Hall

The choir of the Anglican Cathedral
Church of St. John the Baptist

Hasselblad and Pentax 6x7 cameras were used with Kodak films to create all the images.

Printed and bound in Hong Kong by Everbest Printing

Second Printing 1988

Canadian Cataloguing in Publication Data

Ben Hansen 1927-

NEWFOUNDLAND

ISBN 0-9693174-0-9

1. Newfoundland-Description and travel Views. 1 Title